The Step-In Father

Not being the face of the one you replace

Dr. Reynald J. Williams, I

Copyright © 2025 DR. REYNALD J. WILLIAMS, I

Scripture quotations marked (KJV) are taken from the KING JAMES VERSION, public domain. No part of this document may be reproduced or transmitted in any form or by any means, electronic, mechanical, photocopying, recording, or otherwise, without prior written permission of the author.

THE STEP-IN FATHER
Not Being the Face of the One You Replace

Dr. Reynald Joseph Williams
EMAIL reynaldjwilliams@gmail.com

ISBN #978-1-943342-61-7

Printed in the USA.
All rights reserved

Published by: EAGLES GLOBAL BOOKS | Frisco, Texas
In conjunction with the 2022 Eagles Authors Course
Cover & interior designed by DestinedToPublish.com

ACKNOWLEDGMENTS

I wish to express my deepest appreciation to my dear children, Carlos, Teresa, Christopher, Curtis (deceased), Ayondela, Davis, Reynald II, Cecoria, and the host of young men and women God has given me in ministry. To my eighteen grandchildren and my great-grandchildren, for the lessons I have learned through them not only as a father and a stepfather but also as a spiritual father, and for their not judging my numerous shortcomings.

To my brother, Kenneth, for his continued encouragement and counsel when I wanted to quit. To my auntie Bobbie: You don't know how you have touched my life. And to all of my close friends. You know who you are. Thank you for the prayers.

No two individuals are alike. The variables in personality traits present a battle for us all, and a God-centered purposeful relationship is truly a blessing from God. Coupled with the battle within each of us to know our true selves and to allow the Holy Spirit to change our character from carnal to spiritual, we all are a work in progress, and for that reason alone, I am thankful.

Yes, I have failed all my children to a degree; if you think you haven't, the Scriptures prove otherwise. Yet the door is always open for reconciliation. In my imperfections, I have damaged some of them, and for this, I have repented and asked for forgiveness. It took a while for me to realize that I damaged some of their images of what a father and stepfather should look like. Now I can see clearly how I, too, was damaged because I lacked a good, strong male role models in my own life. Let me add that it is never too late to train a child, a teenager, a man, or a woman in the way they should go. But first, each of us must become teachable. You must never forget that you have been hurt, too, and are automatically prone to hurt others. Also, that the child in you is longing for healing, deliverance, and to be made whole. It may come as a surprise, but the people who are in your home right now are your starting points to learn how to be God's answer for the family.

As you maneuver through the pages of this book, take time to reflect. Remember, you cannot be an impactful parent until you seek counsel with the Holy Spirit and confront the demons that you have collected along your life journey. You may want to say, "Except for me," or you may say, "I just can't change." Whatever the poison you have accepted and feed your inner self with, the Spirit of God stands at the door of your hardened heart and is simply asking to be let in. Repent now, for the Kingdom of Heaven is at hand.

CONTENTS

Acknowledgments III

Introduction VII

CHAPTER 1: Who Are You? 1

CHAPTER 2: I'm Going To My Mother's House 18

CHAPTER 3: All By Myself? 35

CHAPTER 4: God Adopted You 49

CHAPTER 5: For The Team 57

Conclusion 71

Scripture References 78

References 83

INTRODUCTION

You don't hear much about the role of stepfathers today. As a matter of fact, you don't see many images of fathers in family leadership positions in the media at all anymore. The focus today seems to be on the single-mother household and on her ability to lead a family without a man. This goes against everything that God teaches for the godly maturation of children: *"And God blessed them, and God said unto them, Be fruitful, and replenish the earth ..."* (Genesis 1:28). Could it be because having a father figure in a home has become a lost necessity in today's social structure, or is it because there are not enough strong, identifiable fatherly role models left for young men to emulate? You decide.

Today, in this 21st century, there are more men and women living in a second or third marriage. Others are choosing to remain single. And what about the raising of the children that come along with that marriage or from premarital sex? What about step-in-mothers? They, too, have mysteriously disappeared from the landscape of life as role models for single-parent families that have risen expeditiously in the social structure. This world system has unwittingly removed the natural father image/matrix from the family format that God created in the beginning. Without much thought, it has begun the removal of God the Father from the family as well. And if there is no God the Father perceived in the mind of humanity, it is easy to remove the purpose of the physical man from the family landscape. Each of us needs to examine this statement and deal with it in the scope of future generations.

Let me add that many of the comments and observations made in the following chapters are not all-inclusive. The intent here is to reveal to you the numerous ways Satan uses a man's vulnerabilities to attack the core of a man's Christian beliefs. As you study each chapter, meditate on the Scriptures and questions at the end. It is my sincere prayer that after you complete the reading of this book, you will become equipped with the spiritual weaponry to combat YOUR spiritual enemy and complete your Kingdom assignment as a step-in-father.

JOSEPH

Given the limited biblical data available, what lessons can we learn from the life of Joseph, Jesus' stepfather? First, *parenting is a critically important, lifelong activity.*

One: *Parenting takes commitment and a strong will to succeed.* When God the Father intended to prepare His Son for earthly ministry, He placed Him under the tutelage of a godly man (flesh). A man who would lead his family in a spirit of humility and submission: "*Then Joseph her husband, being a just man, and not willing to make her a public example, was minded to put her away privily*" (Matthew 1:19). Before going to the second point, read Matthew 1:20 and ask yourself, "Am I hearing from God?"

Two: *Obedience to God involves risk-taking*. The angel's directive to Joseph, to proceed with his marriage plans, contradicted common sense and thus required a deep trust in God and not the traditions of his culture. In other words, Joseph's relationship with God caused him to "*...walk by faith, not by sight*" (2 Corinthians 5:7). The path Joseph was called to follow wasn't "safe," but it fulfilled God's design for the world. Remember this. God never promised you safe passage. But, like Abram, your walk in your marriage—in the spirit and not your flesh—and the spiritual development of your wife and children will reap you great godly dividends in the Kingdom of God.

Three: *We must come to terms with God's authority*. Joseph thought that his perceived holy traditions required him to spurn Mary, but the opposite was true. As we grow in the Lord, we often find that our worldly preconceived attitudes, traditions, and notions—even those pertaining to our Christian beliefs and lifestyle—will be challenged by God.

Four: *Poverty is no barrier to Christian service*. As Joseph was a carpenter—a trade that was apparently valued little in first-century

Palestine, Joseph and Mary's condition was such that they offered two birds as a sacrifice—a protocol specified for those unable to afford a lamb: *"And to offer a sacrifice according to that which is said in the law of the Lord, A pair of turtledoves, or two young pigeons"* (Luke 2:24). Also read Leviticus 12:8. Since God didn't choose a well-to-do man to stepfather Jesus, we can rest assured that our financial limitations won't bar us from impacting our family, our household, our wife, our children, and our neighbors' children for Christ.

Five: *Obedience is the basis for leadership.* Nothing in the biblical record suggests that Joseph was charismatic or flamboyant. His overarching traits were *obedience* and *humility*. He obeyed civil decrees, Old Testament laws, and angelic direction. Because he was willing to submit to every legitimate authority, God entrusted him with a significant leadership role.[1]

He:

1. Heard from God.
2. Treated Jesus as his biological son.
3. Was mild-mannered.
4. Was patient and humble.
5. Didn't force his will on Jesus or Mary.
6. Put his family before his feelings and emotions.

It is interesting to me that few of us have considered the role that Joseph, the step-in-father of our Messiah, played in His life. Just think about it for a minute. Joseph, a carpenter, was engaged to Mary, the mother of our Messiah, when he found out that she was *"with child"*—pregnant (Matthew 1:18). Here spawned two views of the geniality of Joseph's ancestry. Read Matthew 1:16–17 and Matthew 1:18–19. This is food for thought. Matthew 1:19 tells us that *"...Joseph, her husband, being a just man, and not willing to make her a public example, was minded to put her away privily."* The word "minded" here can imply an inward thought, or it can imply that he took counsel with someone on the matter.

Joseph wasn't righteous according to man's standards. If it were us who came into the knowledge of our bride-to-be's condition, we would have gotten rid of the woman and would not have done it privately. Everyone we know would have gotten an ear full of our disgruntled view of *that* woman. It would have been on Facebook, TikTok, Instagram, X, and in the church bulletin. We would paint ourselves, men, as righteous and her as, well, I won't use the word here.

Joseph, however, is called righteous because he lived an upright life before God. He was then called to the step-in-fathership ministry because he walked with God blamelessly and uprightly in the commandments and ordinances of the Lord. This made him a perfect fit to mature Christ in what He needed to learn about the operations of the flesh. I'm not aware of one man today who can make this claim.

Your marriage to your wife is your ministry. Maturing the children God has given you, biologically or in a blended family, is your ministry. It is your primary responsibility moving forward and for the rest of your life.

I believe Joseph's life should be studied by every potential father, step-in or biological, who is contemplating marriage or remarriage because the principles that Joseph sets forth are the blueprint for all fathers to live their lives.

Pastors, youth ministry leaders, and marriage counselors should make Joseph's life relevant to all males twelve years and older in their congregations. I say this because, like Joseph, we are filling the same capacity of fathering that he did. Let me explain. The biological children living in your home and those children that are not your biological children all have one thing in common: They were given to you by God. Please let us not neglect to include those children who were not produced from your seed and are not a part of your household but with whom you come into contact often enough so as to impact their destiny.

Children are given to you to mature and release them back to God. We all know this Scripture: *"Train up a child in the way he should go: and when he is old, he will not depart from it"* (Proverbs 22:6). Children will emulate your actions and behavior. So, watch what you do and say around them at all times. I want you to comprehend what I am saying. Before you release them into the world, you have a spiritual responsibility to release them to God first. Fathers, everything you do, say, don't do, and don't say is having either a positive or a negative impact on your children. The tone in which you do it also impacts them. So, according to Proverbs 22:6, who trained you?

Let's look at some statistics on blended families: How prevalent are stepfamilies?

- 40% of married couples with children (i.e., families) in the US are step couples (at least one partner had a child from a previous relationship before marriage; this includes full and part-time residential stepfamilies and those with children under and/or over the age of 18). The percentage of all married couple households is 35% (Kearney, Garvin, & Thomas, 2003).[2]
- 100 million Americans have a step relationship.
- Approximately one-third of all weddings in America today form stepfamilies.[3]

Across the demographics of the remarriage culture, a gray area of developmental and training of children can hinder a Christ-like blending in a family structure. As this is true with the traditional family matrix of one husband with one wife for life, and the children born to that union, it is more complex for those couples who blend their new family with offspring from a previous marriage or a previous relationship. "The issues of one's past are always attempting to impact the progress in their future and the future of the offspring." Many couples limit their "we're married" to their singular idea of this life event. Merging their differences so that their individuality forms a oneness never seems to become an option for them. They never consider how the impact of negative influences, mistakes, "oops, my bad," and bad practices witnessed by them in their lives from their parents, their guardian, their foster home, their grandparents, their community, or their relationship with their previous mate or spouse forms their present perceptions of marriage.

The social shifting of the family structure, which today goes totally against the Word of God, is creating a serious moral decline in this generation and in the meaning of family. The sad commentary is that the Church has become mute on this very significant subject or, to a small degree, they have embraced it. Social action groups are using media to press their agenda to create their image of "the new age modern family." If the church doesn't stand up now, in a few years, that is exactly what we will have: a secularly modern image of a man-made family, not a God-made one. God, the creator of the family, will be totally removed and forgotten: *"They have dealt treacherously against the Lord: for they have begotten strange children: now shall a month devour them with their portions"* (Hosea 5:7).

The scope of parental influence has taken a back seat to the responsibilities of rearing and raising a child in God's image. Media and the judicial system have given children unprecedented power over their parents, and now the child tells the parent what to do and what not to do. Many parents want to be more sociable with their children and are looked at as friends and not as parents by their children. They totally neglect their responsibility to train their children and fear setting any restrictions on them that—in their opinion—would cause their child to become reclusive toward them and emotionally unstable.

Whatever their child wants, their child gets. Note this: The media tells your children what they want, not you. It will also tell them that they need what the media deems important to them to fit into its world culture, not God's Kingdom. If you are not wise as a godly father, you will set no limit on the potential for them to be raised to become a narcissistic child. Where do you think the selfie comes from? Everybody wants to be seen, and everybody wants to be recognized, heard, and accepted by everyone else. If the attention is not on them, it's not important. Few people accept themselves under the microscope of God, so they remove God from the equation and make their own god(s)—the opinions of ungodly people.

What do you remember about your father, if anything, that matured you? You will see that I used the word "mature" and not "raise." I view *maturing a child* as the power of God in your life. You fully develop him or her in body, mind, and spirit; *You raise corn; you can't train it.* So, as you can see, you raise children when you feed them, clothe them, and provide shelter for them. This is all external. But when you mature them, you develop within them a love for God and the knowledge of who they are in His plan for their lives. Their minds are shifted from carnal (self) to spiritual and from living in man's kingdom to living in the Kingdom of God. They, too, become peculiar to the world's standard of what is accepted as normal behavior. Let them know that they will be bullied, but this is because those who bully them fear them and do not have the desire to know God.

Let's take some time for another look at the role of a "step-in- father." What does God have to say about him, and what is it about God that gives the blueprint for the path that a step-in-father should take toward his children, his wife, his home, and his environment? Finally, as the sub-title suggests: "Don't compete!" You are not the face of the one you replace.

CHAPTER 1

WHO ARE YOU?

I know that these may come off as some strange questions to ask, but they need to be answered truthfully by you right here, right now. There are several points of reference and reality checks that need to be made here.

Are you:

- Single with no children and about to marry a woman with children—whose children's father is in the picture?
- Single with children and are about to marry a woman with children—whose children's father is not in the picture?
- A stepfather who has no authority in his home because your wife doesn't want you correcting, disciplining, or guiding her children?
- A stepfather who receives no respect from his spouse, causing the children to disrespect you as well?

- A stepfather who has disconnected from your leadership role in the household altogether because you feel defeated, and now you have secluded yourself in the "man cave"?
- A stepfather who is finding out that the whole family—including yourself—needs family Christian counseling?
- Not married to a woman with children, but you have made yourself available to mentor her children toward a balanced, God-loving life?

Let me say from the onset that you are not alone. All of us men and our families should seek counsel occasionally. There doesn't need to be a perceived problem, but counseling is a way for you to check yourself and refocus from time to time on what is essential. Remember, as your children mature, their needs and your needs in the relationship will change. It can also reveal some very negative facts about yourself, your spouse, and your children that you or they were unaware of, which could be the root cause of division in your home. Remember, as you, your wife, and the children mature, attitudes about certain aspects of life will slowly change. Without God, and proper counseling, you, she, or they can become skewed. If you don't address these issues before they take root, you can easily find yourself off balance, resulting in behaviors that become more detrimental to you and to the family core. In other words, you unknowingly become the problem and not the problem-solver. Proverbs 20:5 reads: *"Counsel in the heart of man is like deep water; but a man of understanding will draw it out."*

Proverbs 20:18 tells us: *"Every purpose is established by counsel: and with good advice make war."*

You are at war with an enemy that you cannot see and who had been in the business of killing, stealing, and destroying long before you were conceived in your mother's womb. Only through wise, godly counsel can you stand a chance of waging war against him and winning. Remember this. This enemy identifies hidden issues in each of our lives and works tirelessly to uproot God's image in the home and replace it with his own—disobedience, chaos, and confusion. Note that he will use your wife and children to expose the hidden issues that you failed to see, and he will use you to do the same to them. Let this knowledge not be egregious or offensive for you or for them. Always communicate with a supportive posture.

As I stated in my book, *The Garden of Your Mind*,[4] each of us has been impacted by our parents, our grandparents, our aunts and uncles, our cousins, our nieces and nephews, our teachers, our neighbors, our friends, and our enemies, be it naturally or spiritually. All these individuals have planted a core memory in you that may now be a subliminal emotion that acts out destructively when triggered. In short, you have become a mixture of a multiplicity of internalized false images of what a parental role is and what a parent's purpose is. If not brought under control, you may find yourself operating with a carnal and/or a spiritual bipolar disorder and not know it. Today, you are motivated. Tomorrow, you walk around depressed. Gentlemen, have you been honest with yourself? Do you honestly know who you are? Are you aware of your own formed idiosyncrasies that a childhood memory has wedged itself into your core thinking—your subconscious? Do you find yourself reflecting on your past, seeking to find out what went wrong and finding no tools to repair the damage? Do you have unrealistic, preconceived notions about what a marriage is about? Did you consider the seven issues listed above before you got married, or did you do what many of us have done: Just get married to satisfy a physical want, subliminally? Yes, you wanted to get married, but as you will hear stated throughout this book, was the core of your "I DO" predicated on true agape LOVE, which is an action word, or was it predicated on something else? The love of   ; you fill in the blank.

In my counseling with and in general conversation with many men today, as well as women, it is apparent that they are not operating or functioning in the will of God for their life when they believe they have found that one person (of the opposite sex) that can make their life complete. If you are not whole before you enter into marriage, trust me, it will not be achieved after you are married. It only gets worse: a cesspool of continued seeking for validation. You dump your carnal waste on each other to clean up. You are looking for a princess, and she is looking for a knight in shining armor. We live with a fantasy mindset, and a lot of it comes from what we see in media. I am not knocking down social media; however, if you are not honest with yourself, the image in the public eye to many men and women is everything. If you are honest with yourself, many times, your view of yourself is painted on your canvas by an experience that you had with someone you looked up to. It was their paint, not God's.

Now, you find yourself seeking validation from an ungodly/false image of yourself. To some, the fear of living life alone is frightening. Trust me, you live alone with yourself, in your thoughts, feelings, and emotions, far longer than you will live in the presence of another person. The feeling of loneliness can devastate others to the point of receiving *the spirit of possession* of the opposite sex that they are in a relationship with. We are not here to possess an individual; that's demonic. We are here, however, to esteem our mate higher than ourselves. Gentlemen, if you fail to have her know and trust that she is your priority, if you fail to make your children and her children your priority, you fail at being the man God created you to be.

Let's continue in our pursuit of honesty. You tend to focus more on the physical aspects of the relationship—what this woman can do for you physically. There is little or no serious consideration of the spiritual aspects of the relationship, only physicality. You accept and take note of the perceived flaws in her during the courtship of your relationship and honestly believe that you can change this woman into the image you want her to be. Trust me, she is doing the same thing with you. Neither of you realizes that each of you already has a false image of yourself and of each other simply because you both forced yourselves to be on your best behavior during the courtship. You both lied to yourselves and to each other. But wait until the honeymoon is over and the bright light of ecstasy dims. What both of you saw as a saint now looks like a demon, and you are at each other's throats. You no longer see their light; all you see is their darkness. Darkness that both of you hid from each other. Remember Dr. Jekyll and Mr. Hyde?

Gentlemen, she is a woman! Even if she doesn't realize it, her role in the marriage is to *help* you, not *be* you. And this applies to you toward her: "*And the Lord God said, it is not good that the man should be alone; I will make him a help meet for him*" (Genesis 2:18). She has a womb; you have testicles. You are the giver; she is the receiver. If you are not giving her and the children the image of Christ in your life, it will be hard for them to receive you. Yes, she is subject to fight you, but in reality, it's not a fight against you; it's a fight against your imperfections and change. Psalm 51:5 reminds us: "*Behold, I was shapen in iniquity; and in sin did my mother conceive me.*"

Think about this: Even though she may not know it, your wife's main job is to help you become the man God called you to be. Trust me; she has her work cut out for her. You are to help her become the woman God called her to be. Trust me again; your work has also been cut out for you. In other words, as you reflect on her strengths and weaknesses, she is to reflect on your strengths and weaknesses. You do not have the same strengths and weaknesses, and because of that, at the beginning of the courtship process, you admired each other's differences. As the Holy Spirit works on you to smooth out your rough edges, you, too, should be gentle as the Holy Spirit gives you what to pray for in the smoothing out of her rough edges as well.

You should always complement each other because *both of you are bringing what is needed to the table of life and should be enjoying the meal together*. In my next book, *Becoming One*, I'll talk more about the importance of "pillow talk." Patience is the answer for both of you. You have the expanse of your lifetime here on earth, a very small dash (-) with the help of the Holy Spirit to prepare a spiritual table suitable for both you and your children. You can eat from this table without ever becoming spiritually sick. If your family is already sick spiritually and is suffering from spiritual malnutrition because of spiritual diarrhea due to worldly junk food, you need to immediately turn to God's spiritual table of life. Together, you will gather strength day by day to fight off the fiery darts of Satan, mend the damaged area(s) that neither of you were aware of, and gain strength *together* to go back into battle. Keep It Spiritual, Son (KISS). Remember Genesis 2:18. This is a war that you and they will not win alone. They need you to lead.

Too often, however, one or both of you willingly neglect to consider the decayed and rotten attitudes, beliefs, and dispositions that you brought to the table. You don't see your responsibility to seek God in support of each other in removing spiritual decay from your spouse. You just see your spouse's rottenness. STOP here for a few minutes and, honestly, with the aid of the Word of God, look at what is needed from both of you to remove the spots, the wrinkles, and the blemishes from your spouse and from yourself. Remember, work on yourself only. Your spouse has enough challenges working on her own self.

Take a few minutes and meditate on Philippians 2:12b: "... *work out your own salvation with fear and trembling.*" Let your light shine, not a demanding spirit. It may seem to you that I'm focusing on the spouse here, but you are right. Why, you ask? Because, gentlemen, you must remember that as you minister to your biological children the love of God, you must also minister to her children. Children are quick to identify favoritism whether from you or from her. They know what true love feels like too.

Regardless of the situation you may find yourself in your marriage today, gentlemen, YOU have a spiritual responsibility to set the table. Yes, as she may set the physical table for meals and the like, you have the prestigious honor of setting the spiritual table under the guidance of the Holy Spirit. *Too often, we as men are attempting to live our lives through our marriage and forget that we are to lose our lives in our marriage.* Each day, less of you needs to show up at the table and more of Christ in you should be at the table: "*Husbands, love your wives, even as Christ also loved the church, and gave Himself for it*" (Ephesians 5:25). You both are to become more and more like Christ each day. You are also to bear the fruit of love, joy, peace, long-suffering, gentleness, goodness, faith, meekness, and self-control (Galatians 5:22–23a). You are to give your love unconditionally and without any thought of a return on your investment. Read Luke 14:12–14. You may wish to interpret this Scripture as one preparing a meal for others. This applies to you as well. Remember, prepare the table, and look for nothing in return. Christ is your reward. You should be seeking an eternal return, not a physical one, remembering that your reward is spiritual, not carnal. I know this may sound strange to you, but the best gift you can give to your family is your fleshly (carnal-natured) death. If you don't, your wife and the children will know it, and you will find yourself alienated in the flesh and in the spirit by them. They will be in the house, but that house will not be a home.

You are to love your wife and children with all of their faults and shortcomings, realizing that you also have faults and shortcomings. Please note that it is extremely easy to focus on others' faults while ignoring your own. The reason for this is that when you look at the shortcomings of others, you are looking at them from the outside of their life experiences. When it comes to you looking at your own shortcomings, you are on the inside failing to sense the gravity of your actions on those outside of yourself. Your tunnel vision is focused outwardly, never inwardly. You can visually see others' faults as they are directed toward you, but you fail to see your own faults as they are directed toward others because you don't take the time to look within yourself and line your behavior up with the Word of God. You don't take your mess seriously or its negative impact on your ministry to your family and others. You may even become shocked when a negative behavior is revealed to you by your spouse or children. You just ignore it. Why not? They don't know you, right? They are to live for you, right? Wrong.

If you had not focused so much on the few good characteristics about your spouse, but more on her multiplicity of shortcomings, would you have married her? Please note I said, "few good characteristics." Would she have married you if she had not focused more on the few good characteristics about you but had focused more on your shortcomings? I don't think so, but you are married now, and both of you should sit at the table God has prepared for you and consume the much-needed fruit that will bring healing to your soul, your mind, and your marriage. Remember, all of this is for the kids. Be willing to PILLOW TALK with each other DAILY with an open heart about the things that you and she are doing that rock the boat. Don't look at it as "I'm being controlled"; look at it as "I'm being set free of my flesh; I'm being purged." Pillow talk is the ability to talk to each other all day long in a whisper. You become the cool breeze blowing through her emotions, continuously bathing her in the comfort of the healing power of God. Yes, all day! She is to do the same for you.

You are to extol your wife every day of her life. You should have joy. This joy stems not from what and who your wife is in your mind's eye today. Your joy comes in knowing that as you love her unconditionally, you are in great anticipation of God's will in her life to mold her and shape her into the woman He has called her to be in Him, not the woman you imagine or want. With the correct and insightful godly guidance from the Holy Spirit, all of her spots, wrinkles, and blemishes are removed. Because of your eternal love for her and the children, you gently rub them away. The same attitude should apply to her for you. Both of you are long-suffering, realizing how Christ suffered for you. You become fully aware of the task that each has in bringing your own selves into oneness with each other as you become one in Christ. You are gentle with her because she is the weaker vessel and needs to be handled tenderly—not like an old hubcap to be thrown away because it has some rust on it and some dents in it. Remember, even a rusted and dented hubcap can be restored to its former luster. Until then, roll with what you have and allow God to do the restoring; you are not equipped for it because He also wants to restore you. Why? Because He created you and her in His image. Stop trying to recreate each other in your image. The Holy Spirit is the rust and dent remover. Not you.

You should—without ceasing—encourage her to be the best wife, the best mother, and the best woman she can be for the glory of God, not for you (Proverbs 31:10–31). And let us not forget, she is to be your best friend. Your nature should be filled with goodness toward her, for your desire is for her to have a better end in Christ. You work at finding only the good in her, and you build her up in those areas, not speaking of your perceived shortcomings in her life. *You are always positive about her potential, not fault-finding about her failures.* You maximize her holy parts to the fullest. You have undying faith in her, realizing that she is not perfect but is being perfected. You trust in God's ability and not your own, and this keeps you meek and humble. Remember Joseph. You put Christ first in all your decisions for the emotional and spiritual development of your home. You are not in control, because you have given all control to God.

This attitude in your life and in the life of your marriage is subject to not fitting in with the normal way of doing marital business in the world market today. On the other hand, you have made up your mind to transact all your business from the marketplace of God's Kingdom. You are purposeful in the alleys, the courts, the circles, the avenues, the boulevards, the streets, the roads, the highways, the byways, and the expressways of life as you travel with your family, keeping the children your main focus. You rise early each day, serving your family with prayer and ensuring that all potholes, hidden nails, and roadblocks are removed from their daily life walk so that nothing can deflate the plans God has for you and for them. You are "God's man"! Repeat after me, "I am God's man!" Your wealth is not in terms of how much money you make, how fine you think you are, or in the things that you possess. Your wealth is centered on the spiritual maturation of your household—that wife and those children God has privileged and favored you to steward with a life-impacting opportunity of mercy and grace. God and I want you to know that your marriage is "FRAGILE; HANDLE WITH CARE."

As you loved this gift, this woman, throughout the courtship, you have a God-ordained responsibility to spiritually plant and water her with the Word of God daily so that she grows strong and matures into "The Body of Christ." Let me reiterate a previous point again. Each of you has removed the facade that hides (Hyde) the true you. She and you are fighting past images. It is your painful past image of each other that keeps you from immersing yourself in each other's godly potentials. Yes, it will cost you your life, for *the true godly fruit that is buried in you must die first before it can stimulate spiritual growth in the soul that you call "WIFE."* As you well know, any male who obtains the ability to copulate can be an instrument to bringing a child into this world, but it takes a special man, a godly man, to aid in birthing them and his household into the Kingdom of God.

You are probably wondering why I'm spending so much time on the wife when this book is about the step-in-father. Great observation. If you look closely, as I have talked briefly about the wife, I have also structured a foundation for the step-in-father to build on. It is my prayer that you will begin to experience a deeper and more profound addiction to the lifelong spiritual improvement of your marriage situation and remember that God has given you all the tools you need—*in His Word*—to repair (tuck-point) any structural damage thrown at you by the evil one, created by the past life experience of you, your spouse, and your (step)child(ren).

As you complete each chapter, take a few minutes to ask yourself, "Who am I?" The reason I say this is because each day of your life, you should be changing more and more into the husband and the step-in-father you have been called to be as a Godman in Christ, not only in your home but in your community as well. All children who visit your domain on this earth should receive a word of encouragement from you and your wife, enabling them to see the fullness of the love that God has for them. *Remember, if they don't see it in you, you make it difficult for them to see it in God.*

GROUP DISCUSSION QUESTIONS

General Discussion Questions (for whole groups)

1. What is the general teaching you received growing up about manhood?
2. What is the general teaching you grasped in this chapter?
3. What changes do you need to make in response to the lesson this week (in actions, mindset, etc.)?
4. What are some of the constraints that hold you back from living a life that is impactful in the life of a child that is not biologically yours?
5. In what ways do you see the Church entangled in the ways and values of the world?
6. In your own words, explain why so many men entering into a blended-family marriage miss addressing the eight points of reference discussed in this chapter. What can you do to equip the sons in your life and community for this spiritual assignment in marriage?

Personal Application Questions (for breakout groups)

1. What did the Lord impress upon your heart as you read this chapter?
2. In the description of the husband given in Ephesians 5:25, which aspect of this type of ministry is most appealing to you?
3. Which is the hardest thing for you to believe could happen to you in marriage? Why?

4. The step-in-father life requires shedding things you cherish and changing your priorities and disciplines. How does that make you feel?

5. Are you ready for this ministry called marriage?

6. How can you pray for one another to get to the place with God that each of you is being called to?

Weekly Prayer Target:

1. Spend an extended amount of time in prayer this week. First, spend a few moments in silence listening to what God is speaking to your heart. How will you answer His call? Then, spend more time listening.

2. Cry out in honesty before God. Ask Him to work deeply in your life to do what you cannot do for yourself.

3. What have you discovered about yourself that reveals a change in your thinking that needs to take place?

PRAYER

Heavenly Father, I pray for a Spiritual revival in my life as I pursue to be the Godman that You have called me to be in my relationship with You, my wife, and our (step)child(ren). Help me, Lord, to identify who I am in You as You lead me onto the path to reveal the path that each of our children is to take in You. Help me to discern the flaws in my thinking and in theirs so that I may, through Your perfect will for me, become an example of Your tender love and mercy in the natural to them. Show me how to be a true friend, husband, and father. In Jesus' name, Amen!

CHAPTER

2

I'M GOING TO MY MOTHER'S HOUSE

Let's take a few minutes to look at the above statement. Too often, this statement is made by children and young adults who visit their parents. You tend not to hear them say, "I'm going to my father's house," or "I'm going to my parents' house." In most cases, the statement is: "I'm going to my mother's house." Why do you think this is? It may have its reasoning hidden behind a specific agenda. I have paid attention to the commercials played throughout this age on radio and television. Women are said to be the biggest consumers of all products on the planet. Even if a man buys the product, it tends to be for the home, and society says that the home is the woman's domain. It makes one wonder if the Church is preparing herself to receive the Kingdom of God, or, has she, like sheep, in the world, wandered off into a field full of wolves? Even the Church has become a domain for women. Just a thought. I'm not here to debate. Just to observe.

I buy my own clothes; however, women always ask me if my wife bought them for me as if I don't have a qualified taste in clothing and I need my wife to validate my eye for fashion. I know many of them are joking, but this little harmless jest, like others, can reflect the subtle ideas held by some women and some men, and by media and the marketplace. Gentlemen, if a society woman believes that you are not able to buy yourself a pair of dress slacks, a dress or casual shirt, or a neatly organized pair of socks and shoes, then you are at the mercy of your wife or your significant other to coordinate your wardrobe for you. If you are not observant, it could escalate into the coordination of your life. Without realizing it, some may be looking at you as if you are a child and you need Mommy to dress you correctly. You don't lead; she does. I'm not saying that all men have the talent to coordinate a wardrobe. I am saying, however, that as the attention of this world shifts to highlight women in a dominating imagery way, Christian men, in general, have been placed in the same category as other men of the world have been placed in. A disposable commodity.

Due to the challenges that mothers have with work, maturing children, and balancing the affairs of the family, the role of the husband is sometimes limited to that of being a cash cow or a sperm donor. In either case, the role of the husband is diminished. You can provide, but you can't lead; you can give input, but you can't be the head. You are the provider and nothing more. Your spiritual guidance plays second fiddle to the wishes of Mom. MOM RULES. I believe Genesis 3:16

sums it up: "... *and thy desire shall be to thy husband* ..." Gentlemen, it is a woman's nature to usurp your God-given authority, and they are not aware of it. Part of this problem stems from the fact that many of us men are clueless about how to minister in a household. It is something that has not been purposely taught. We are more prone to fighting physically and emotionally against our spouse in an attempt to show our manhood, only to miss the spiritual meaning of how a godly man matures his home. To that end, you must ask yourself this question: What is God asking me to do? The answer is simple. "LOVE!" Oh, by the way, that is the first commandment (Mark 12:30–31). In order to be a great lover, you have to put all feelings, thoughts, and emotions about you to death. Everything that you do from this moment on revolves around you being the covering for your household—the gatekeeper. *They must feel protected by you and not afraid of you.*

Civil law is now pushing out God's plan and replacing it with its own carnal agenda. As stated in the previous chapter, even the children have more rights than you. However, many men in our churches have misinterpreted and misused God's plan in relationships and marriage to the detriment of the male species. They lead like barbarians and not like saints. As more of the world's view filters into the Church, many men and women in the faith have developed tunnel vision to the reality of Satan's scheme to dominate her and you, canceling out your God-given purpose to serve God and not yourselves. As this country was being formed, many plantation owners used this Scripture, Genesis

9:25, to promote the slavery of Africans stolen and brought to North America. Because of fear and insecurity, men have used Genesis 3:16b. Instead of treating women as equals, we have treated them as slaves, subordinates. In many cases, we have been abusive and cruel solely on the premise that we are (were) the sole providers. If this is the case for you, you are operating in your carnal nature and not your godly nature.

Some of this can be attributed to the nurturing impact that mothers naturally possess, coupled today with the absence of godly fathers in the home to bring balance. When she carries a child till delivery, there is a bond formed. She has brought a life into the world. She felt it kick and stretch in her womb. She heard its heartbeat, and, through the technology of the ultrasound, she was able to see this child—her angel—develop in her womb. Unbeknown to her, she may have become somewhat possessive. It tends to manifest itself with the firstborn, the last born, and/or a son. Children, however, learn at an early age how to use this nurturing spirit against the authority of the step-in-father, resulting in a greater negative spirit against the authority of the father. Depending on the age of the child(ren), this new person in the household, you, sleeping with their mother, can pose a problem for the attention they seek. They may not even have paid that emotion much attention, but because you are there now, it is highlighted, and they will find ways to draw her attention away from you. Both of you must see the signs and nip them in the bud. Together, you two must stop it before it gets established and takes root. It is a subtle act, and some children will have no idea of what they are doing. They will just want Mommy's attention.

You, on the other hand, may be so focused on being the provider that you are absent from the home more than being there, and when you are there, you are a recluse. You are tired or hungry, or you have made other plans for time alone in the home. Not only is the honeymoon over for you and your spouse but there is also an alienation effect on the children. There is a greater negative impact against the step-in-father simply because you failed your primary ministry of continuous connectedness through undying positive communication. They never will get to know you as a person or your heart if they don't know you or your heart. When the power source is disconnected from the source that needs the power to shine, there will be no light. Can you hear the crickets? Please stay connected to the light source, Jesus Christ, in order to be that conduit in your home (John 8:12, Matthew 5:14). Staying plugged into Jesus will ensure your light is never dimmed or extinguished.

Boys tend to want all of their mother's attention simply because she tends to be more of a nurturer than you. In their mind, "You are my mother's friend." You are not a necessity for them in the household, and in some cases, they have been told by their mother, or someone else, that they are the man of the house. With that mindset, they feel that no other male (man) is required in the home. So, now you become the enemy. *How you and her handle this together at the beginning of the engagement and in the first six months of the union will determine your role in their family, not yours.* Yes, I said, "their family." You could potentially be the outsider looking in on something that is not ordained by God: A Jezebel spirit (1 Kings 18:4), and Delilah (Judges 16; 17). Not in the wife necessarily, but in the children and in you. In today's society, many men compromise their leadership role in the house and retreat to their man cave to maintain their mental peace. Yes, I said "house" because if you and your wife are not of one accord, you do not have a home. I'm quite sure you will agree that anything with two heads is an abomination, and there are many blended marriages (families) today fitting that description.

Wellington Boone in his book *Your Wife Is Not Your Mama* marks Chapter 3 with the title, "Women Should Only Marry Grown-up Me."5 I personally find that title interesting. Why? Because so many men reflect the image of a wife on either the image they have of their own mother or an image they may have had of a friend's mother. The problem with this is when you focus completely on the outside appearance of your mate and fail continuously to focus on your God man, you have already failed. Boone states, "When a man finds a woman, he wants to marry, he had better forget about being so immature as to focus only on her physical appearance. He needs to start thinking about being like Jesus."6 Gentlemen, it will always boil down to you. Remember, when Eve and Adam sinned in the garden by eating the forbidden fruit, God wasn't looking for Eve. He looked for Adam (the man). The sad commentary for that whole passage of Scripture is that not only did Adam blame Eve for his action and failure to be obedient, but he also blamed God. He never saw the iniquity (a sin that involves a deliberate and conscious choice to disobey God's commandments or to harm others) he birthed into the world. Remember, gentlemen, Eve was beguiled (deceived); Adam rebelled. As interesting as these words are, men miss their meaning because they already *think* they are *mature*. They, however, neglect the importance of having mature thoughts, and if they don't, they will always have excuses tucked away to justify their immaturity. Let me explain. Genesis 2:24 reads, "*Therefore shall a man leave his father and his mother, and shall cleave unto his wife: and they shall be one flesh.*"

ONE FLESH

Gentlemen, after you get married, it is your specific responsibility to establish your home under the rulership of God. It is one thing to visit your father and mother's home to seek marital advice; however, you must remember this: The life experiences that your parents had in their time together are not the experiences that you are about to have in your marriage today. The social environment may seem to be the same, but it has changed dramatically. Each generation has experienced the same yet different events of chaos. As life may have been hard for them, it will be harder for you. The social landscape alone is different. If you don't believe me, STOP here for a minute, and read and meditate on 2 Timothy 3:1–5.

If you don't remember anything else that is written in this book, remember this: Marriage is about the blending of two totally different personalities and social backgrounds as well as different beliefs, behaviors, habits, realities, and levels of spiritual maturity into a single unit of oneness that puts God above themselves. That oneness is never about you; nor is it about her. It is all about both of you uniting to becoming *one in* Christ. This is a lifelong pursuit that both of you must focus on, understand, and be committed to so that your purpose for living here on this earth in an eternal union is to become *one in* Christ together and not filled with biting the carnal distractions of life. Nevertheless, for any children brought into that union, be it from the natural process or for the sake of the title of this book, their spiritual maturity will be affected because of what they see you focused on.

So, if you love your mother, yes, she will have a tremendous impact on your thinking. You must now, however, be willing to let Mom go and learn all you can about this other person of the opposite sex who you now call *wife*. How you minister to her, openly and behind closed doors, will brand a picture in the minds of your children. They will know when you have brought hurt or when you have brought joy to her heart. Please read Ephesians 5:25. Why is it, gentlemen, that we will listen to every other woman around us and take their advice but fail miserably to listen to the one we have chosen to become one flesh with?

Here is something to think about. Every husband and wife who has stepchildren must come to the realization that as you are not the biological parent, those children may not like you. But these are exciting times for you. Ephesians 6:4 tells you, *"And ye fathers, provoke not your children to wrath: but bring them up in the nurture and admonition* [authoritative counsel or warning] *of the Lord."*

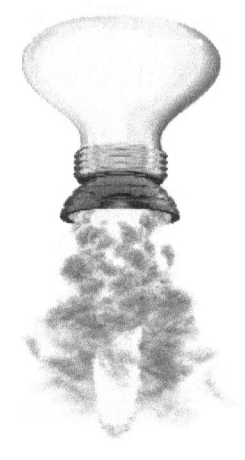

Your role as a stepfather or, for that matter, a biological father, is not to dominate your children. Your role is to guide with all humility and mature your children into the image of God. But that can't happen if you haven't matured into the Godman you are called to be.

So often, in a man's attempt to be called the head of the house, he succumbs to being the devil in the house. He focuses on what his demands are for the household collectively, totally neglecting the true needs of each individual in the house. I want you to note here that the word "home" isn't used again. This is even more egregious to the stepfather who operates in the spirit of man and not in the Spirit of God. Remember, many stepchildren will have issues with you giving them instructions. The truth that you need to accept is that you are not their biological father, and they will always—even if they don't realize it—long for him. I know that it isn't your desire to fill his spot. You can't. You are trying to carve out your own existence with them. But you now have the awesome responsibility to be the image of God in that house and work diligently to make it a home. You are the step-in-father. You have become a filler of the void that many children are faced with today and don't realize they have or need filled.

Did you know that how you look at a child in a one-on-one can invoke a positive or negative response? Now is not the time to nurture your ideas, your feelings, and your emotions like your mother did when you would come home hurt. You have to learn how to nurture through the conflict that your stepchildren are experiencing. Just like you have the responsibility to live with your wife according to knowledge, you also have the responsibility to mature in a way that understands each of the children's physical, mental, and spiritual needs. This is why you have to mature. You cannot mature your stepchildren if you, too, are not mature enough to possess and process a compassion for their spiritual need(s).

OLD FURNITURE MADE NEW

Natalie Nichols Gillespie made an interesting statement in her book *The Stepfamily Survival Guide*. She says, "Parents who have experienced the death of a spouse or have gone through a divorce often overburden the stepfamily trying to make up for the loss, attempting to give each member everything he or she wants. Children and adults need time simply to be. Each family member needs time at home to experience being together in the new household. Stepfamilies constantly on the go add unnecessary stress to the marriage and the family unit. Never forget that if there is any spiritual tuckpointing that needs to be done in the home, it must start with you."7

Generally, when you move into a brand-new house, you buy some new furniture for every room. However, this is not the case when it comes to the gain of a new household. You and your spouse did not acquire her children together; nor did you acquire yours together. You came together after the fact. And even if you give birth to a child or children after the move, the issue of unity will always be walked on a very thin line. Remember, as you and your wife have come together from two separate and independent backgrounds and life experiences, your stepchildren, too, are experiencing separate and independent backgrounds in accordance with their now limited ability to comprehend what reality is verses their feelings and emotions.

As with the children, you, too, suffer somewhat of a loss when you marry. You are no longer in your father and mother's house, where your mother is still cleaning your room, fixing your food, and cleaning your soiled clothing. Hmm, sounds like what you expect your wife to do, doesn't it? Awe, great memories. Or, you may have spent some time as a bachelor, and with that lifestyle, you may have become possessive of (your) stuff. But now the wake-up call. You cannot allow world standards of relationships to redefine God's standard. Now, as a stepfather, you have been charged by God to work out your own salvation (Philippians 2:12) and allow your wife and your stepchildren to work out theirs with some guidance from you. I said some! Here is where wisdom comes in.

With the power of the Holy Spirit, you and your wife need to work daily to remove the poisons that have festered in your spirit. Are you aware that they exist? If you two do not identify and cut out the root of the rotting spiritual cancer, you will find yourselves continuously drained and at each other's throats. Let me explain. Satan will always work in your subconscious to bring up thoughts of your previous relationship, bring up those small failures that resulted in its demise, and bring up *old furniture*. Let us not forget how quickly he will remind you of a recent heated discussion—ok, argument—that you had with your wife. You combat this, with your spouse, by staying in the Word of God, praying together without ceasing, and communicating daily about your feelings, your fears, your dreams, and your family concerns, bringing in *new furniture* (united godly habits) and discarding *old, used furniture* (destructive individual habits). Remember, never be critical, but always be supportive. Never be a complainer, but always be an encourager. Never stab each other in the vulnerable areas that you opened up to each other for discussion. YOU CAN DO THIS.

How do I know? Because you are created in God's image. *God doesn't condemn; He frees.*

THE WATCHMAN

Who was Ezekiel? "Unlike the pre-exilic prophets, whose ministry was primarily to either Judah or the ten-tribe kingdom, Ezekiel is the voice of Jehovah (Ezekiel 3:17) to *"the whole house of Israel."* He is the watchman for the *whole house* of Israel. Your house is brought together by blending two families together. Like Ezekiel, you have the breathtaking responsibility to express the glory of God for your family by working with them to submit to His will for their lives as you, too, submit your life to Him. The whole house. Your leadership as the family watchman, its gatekeeper, is to seek the face of God and allow Him to give you a panoramic view of your family's spiritual condition and to blow the shofar of war against all spiritual and natural enemies that you see seeking to penetrate the walls of protection (Ezekiel 8:9). You are the family lookout, and you must raise the banner of peace daily, bringing your family together to quench the fiery darts of the enemy. Guard your family with your life. Be bold in speaking God's truth to them, not your opinion or personal view.

You have to accept the fact that you no longer have a physical father or mother to protect you, but you do have a God who can, and He will. God wants to show you how to build a house into a home in which He can dwell. He wants to heap His blessings on you and your home, but you have to accept and embrace the fact that God has given you the power to show your family how to open the door to Him as you become the blueprint for their transformation. You are now the *harbinger* for your household, and God is depending on you to mature into the man that will hear His voice and warn them of His coming. You have to become the example of the change that they need to make as they see Him dramatically making changes in you. You also must be cognizant of the fruit that is growing in the minds and hearts of your family. Just because you are in love with this woman who happens to have children, and she loves you, your war will be against all spiritual strongholds, the emotions, and the feelings that her children have toward you, which they will not be able to, or will simply refuse to, express and work through. In some cases, they are not even aware of them. You have to *come out of your emotions and feelings and walk in the anointing of discernment.*

GROUP DISCUSSION QUESTIONS

General Discussion Questions (for whole groups)

1. At times, do you see your mother in your wife?
2. At times, do you wish your wife were as attentive to you as your mother?
3. Have you truly served your wife and family in a way that helps them trust your leadership? Explain.
4. Are you showing a protective and covering atmosphere for your home? Does your family feel safe and secure?
5. Give some examples of ways that the Western culture has negatively impacted the Christian faith in you, your wife, and the children, and how you can combat its effects.

Personal Application Questions (for breakout groups)

1. What are some steps that you need to take to bring your wife, your stepchildren, and your children into a family relationship that God would be well pleased with?
2. One problem impacting blended families is potential reminders of negative experiences that one spouse or the other lived through, or that the children did. Give several steps that you could take to ensure comfort for yourself and for your household if a situation or negative feeling from the past toward a previous spouse or relation comes up. Remember, your seemingly harmless action could stir

up that feeling. The refurbishing of old negative experiences into new positive ones takes continued open communication.

3. Explain why it is important for you to take the lead in praying daily with your wife, with your children individually, with the family collectively, and alone.

Weekly Prayer Target:

1. Pray for the spirit of discernment to separate your view of your wife from the view of your mother.

2. Pray for ways that the Holy Spirit can use you and your wife to become one flesh from a spiritual perspective in Christ and not only in the bedroom.

3. Seek God's face for wisdom to dissolve the fears that you and your wife may have regarding hints of past hurts that could be either prevalent or false in your marriage.

4. Daily ask God, as you study the Scriptures, to reveal to you your full role of being the watchman for your family's spiritual maturity.

5. Remember, it is never about you.

PRAYER

Heavenly Father, I thank You for entrusting me to pastor this household. As You did with Ezekiel, help me, Lord, to stay in the watchtower and view from a long distance all household dangers that are sure to pursue us collectively and individually. Lord, keep me from losing my focus on this breathtaking earthly assignment, and keep me away from biting the carnal distractions that the enemy will sling at the ear and eye gates of my family. Show me, Lord, how to not talk to them from a position of authority, but give me the words and the tone that will give them the zeal to follow You as I do. You are my God. Show me how to bring them into our fellowship together. In Jesus' name, I pray. Amen!

CHAPTER 3

ALL BY MYSELF?

Aloneness is presence, fullness, aliveness, the joy of being, and overflowing love. You are complete. Nobody is needed; you are enough. Love makes you complete. In true relationships, you share with each other, not out of need, but rather as a result of your overflowing energy to be one in Christ.

Loneliness is sadness because one has no friends or company:8 feeling sad and unhappy about being socially isolated.

Love makes you complete because God is love. Loving the God in you where you are right now is key to loving others. In Matthew 22:37–40, Jesus said to a Pharisees' lawyer, *"Thou shall love the Lord thy God with all thy heart, and with all thy soul, and with all thy mind. This is the first and great commandment. And the second is like unto it, Thou shalt love thy neighbor as thyself. On these two commandments hang all the law and the prophets."*

Do you truly know God? How can you impactfully love a woman's child(ren) and expect her to love your child(ren) if neither of you has the love of God resonating in your spirit? So, are you experiencing your relationship with your blended family (your wife and her children) out of your loneliness, or are you experiencing it out of the commandment of God? Look at your level of love like this: If you constantly find fault with yourself—your looks, weight, behavior, lack of social skills, and the list goes on and on—you will unconsciously deem yourself lonely. But it becomes easier to shift the blame to your wife, the kids, and the family simply because you refuse to accept the truth about yourself. You look to them for help and not God.

DR. JEKYLL AND MR. HYDE

Dr. Henry Jekyll is the relationship you want everyone to see in you. Mr. Edward Hyde is the one who you really are. But let's look deeper. Taking the "y" out of Hyde and replacing it with the letter "i," we have the word "hide."

Have you looked seriously at the unknown hidden secular urges that have thrust you into this marriage? You know what I mean? A marriage that allows you to express your urges without feeling guilty and having spiritual consequences for the Hyde side of your nature. Now, as your Hyde side is revealed and you war with him daily, you have a problem with the Hyde side that is found in your wife. Yes, she has one too. For this point, the Hyde side is the sin nature. You have them; you have either embraced them, diligently fought against them, or been appalled by them. Ephesians 2:8 reads, "*For by grace are ye saved through faith; and that not of yourselves; it is the gift of God.*" You sometimes alienate yourself from your wife and family because Satan keeps your past before you in your subconscious, and you feel helpless to change your thinking. You feel hopeless, lost, and alienated. You feed on your past bitter sins. Remember, the whole house is at war with the same nature and feelings of themselves.

As Dr. Jekyll describes himself as Mr. Hyde after murdering Sir Danvers, a godly husband's marriage to his Hyde personality will commit spiritual murder on his wife and stepchildren, which will cause genocide in his household, creating a potential *generational curse* and/or a *spiritual stronghold* that can last for several generations. You willfully move into that tight cubicle that Satan has built for you, and you feel squeezed, outcast, and alone. Your own self-made cell. You have convinced yourself that no one understands the life pressures that you experience every day; nor are they able to comprehend your pain, so you fail to face them due to your fears. Nor have you talked to your help meet about them. You prejudicially hide (Hyde) them. And in time, the pressure will cause you to explode in a symphony of rage and hate. Too many of us are not loving God inwardly or ourselves enough in order to love others outside of our ourselves. *We H(i)yde.*

LOVE

Trust me when I say, "Your kind of love has everything to do with it." Everything about you must be wrapped up in God's love. Remember, aloneness is presence, fullness, aliveness, the joy of being, and overflowing love.

Your wife, your job, your children, your stepchildren, your looks, and yes, even your shortcomings are not the things that should make you, you. Only God can complete you. Again, I say that many of us husbands entered into our marriages expecting to get something out of them. If you are honest with yourselves, God wasn't in the picture. Hyde was in control. On the other hand, we should have entered into our marriages to honor God's plan with the single purpose of giving without expecting anything in return. This is ministry. Marriage is ministry. Outward appearances can be deceiving because, as you may have hidden agendas, she, and her children, independently, have some that are not centered on *love* (God). Your relationship is all centered on the material. The reason I say this is:

1. You had a superficial prayer life in your courtship. You sought God as it benefited your lust. Your Dr. Hyde image. Your self-centeredness caused you not to see the bigger picture. You wanted to keep the children in the den.

2. Your time with the children is more physical, like a pinch of a shoe being too tight on a foot (painful for you and for them). Everyone is experiencing some pain.

3. In your time with the children, you never took time to know them (develop a positive, godly relationship with them) in the courtship phase. All of your interest was solely directed at the woman (it was you, her, then them). It never crossed your mind to put God in the equation.

4. You felt intimidated by her affections toward her children, and you had a hidden desire to have those affections shift to you. Of course, in your mind, you are now the alpha male. You want dominance but fail to see the significance of surrendering that dominance to God. You love yourself, not God.

I had an experience with God that I would like to share with you, if you don't mind. I realize that the world system of doing things is to fill your time up with materialistic activity: the job, the demands of the Church, television, computers, cell phones and all the apps that work with them, sports, parties, and the list goes on and on. I was so consumed by these things that I was literally burned-out. I was overworked and stressed. I was buried in the cesspool of a secular life, and I was good at it. The reason for this stemmed from my childhood. I was deemed ugly by my peers; I was dark-skinned, and my head was out of proportion with my body type. I had zits and pimples really badly as a teenager. I was called Frankenstein and Crater Face. I was awkward, and in my mind I felt like a jinx. The biggest of all was that I wet the bed. All of these temporary shortcomings in my young life were gigantic to me at the time and pressed heavily on my self-esteem as an adult. I had an identity crisis.

It took counseling to help me see this, for this view of myself impacted every relationship with a woman that I pursued. My lack of socialization skills due to my bed-wetting and a fear of the dark which brought on my bed-wetting crippled my ability to feel anything positive about myself. If it went wrong, it had to be my fault. Not only that, but I also over-imposed my shortcomings on anyone (female) who liked me.

I was a wreck, like a ship that had run upon some rocks in a storm, like the Titanic. *I had a hole in my life that hindered me from catching the anointed winds of God, and I had lost all of my spiritual cargo.* By not knowing how to address my fears—and fear is only of the Devil—I was in a vicious cycle of hurting others and being hurt by them. Relationships started out good on the physical side but failed miserably on the spiritual relationship side, with remorse and callous emotional attacks by both parties. What I found out was that I had to move away from my feelings and emotions of being alone and embrace aloneness. My healing started when I stopped blaming others for my internal issues and began to look to God for answers. *My time alone with God helped me to embrace aloneness.*

When I did this, He brought me to the realization that I was not alone because I had figured out that all of my alone time with Him equipped me to address the world outside of myself.

The second thing that helped me was what I found out when I started talking to other men: I wasn't alone in my mindset. All of us men are struggling with something, but we have been taught that men don't have problems; we solve them. When men don't face their fears, their demons, and their dysfunctional feelings and emotions, they raise the welcome sign for Satan to wreak havoc on their lives, internally and externally. When men come together and discuss a marital subject, it is almost always addressed in a carnal way and not in an attempt to bring a spiritual solution. Your spouse and the kids are always the problem, and if we see a problem in ourselves, it's because they won't listen to us. It took time for me to first realize that I was okay, then to feel comfortable by myself and spend more time in the presence of God by myself. This allowed me to listen to the ungodly thoughts that entered my thinking process and call them out.

Remember now, I'm by myself trying to get closer to God, but *my thoughts are louder than my prayers*. Everyone has some type of formed skeleton in their closet. It's like being in a room full of people, but you feel like you are all alone. There is no one present, and you are on your own. When your mind thinks like this, you lose the ability to crucify your flesh and be born to the Spirit of God. You become self-centered and, if you are not careful, you can become self-righteous. The problem here is you will have convinced yourself that you are neither.

Your loneliness stems from the specific reality you wish to live in. The world (physically), your mind (mentally), and not in the Spirit of God. The first two have no redemptive power, but the latter one does. This is why, now, you must seek the latter reign of God in your life. If you choose to live in the world, you are operating in the domain of Lucifer (Satan) (James 4:4). Without Christ in your life, you are doomed to fail. Your next choice is your mind. Here, you run the risk of also being doomed to fail. Your mind is where the battleground for your soul is fought. I address this in my book *The Garden of Your Mind*.[9] It is ongoing and never-ending while you live in your flesh. How do I know this? It happened to Jesus: "*And when the devil had ended all the temptation, he departed from him for a season*" (Luke

4:13). Can you believe it? Jesus was attacked by Satan throughout His ministry here on earth.

So, as this battle is going on in your mind, can you imagine what is going on in the mind of your wife and those children who are not yours, who do not know you, and who really may not want to get to know you? However, here you have a battle that you can win, but you have to come out of your feelings and emotions and surrender to the Spirit of God in order to do it. Note in the above Scripture that the devil left Jesus alone for a *season*. As he is relentless in his attacks on you, your wife, and your children, you have to be relentless in your family prayer time, Bible study, and godly counseling you give to the household. Be willing to receive the wise counsel that your spouse, and sometimes your children, gives you, too. There are no vacations in ministry. You are in it to win it. You are in it until death do you part.

If you choose to stay alone, you will fail. But if you take the time to equip your team (your family) with the tools, skills, and a strong, godly foundation, no weapon that Satan forms against you and them will prosper (Isaiah 54:17). As an overcomer, you can now rejoice over the lives God has placed in your capable hands to mature into strong, godly men and women. Trust me, after they leave the nest, you will be their co-counselor for life, working with the Holy Spirit to keep them focused on holy living. Be the stream they can draw from.

PRAYER

Heavenly Father, I come to You now with a repenting heart, asking for Your forgiveness for my carnal actions that failed in the ministry of being a godly step-in-father. Now, I seek the guidance of Your Spirit as I work to render my whole life to Your will. As I go through the withdrawal of my carnal nature, I need Your Spirit to lead me on the path that I need to go on. Order my steps, Father, and direct me as we put my flesh to death, and I open myself to the full anointing that You have given me. I want to be the kind of step-in-father that You are to all of Your children. I thank You, Jesus, for showing me the path that I must take to bring glory and honor to Your name. I forgive myself for missing the mark and submit myself to You. In Jesus' name, Amen.

GROUP DISCUSSION QUESTIONS

General Discussion Questions (for whole groups)

1. Now that you know, will you combat the feeling of loneliness and guard against its pull in your home?
2. Examine and explain why you hide behind your past and have refused to confess your deliverance from it.
3. What tools will you use, as you are delivered and made whole?
4. What different tools will you use to assist your family in receiving their deliverance, their healing, and their wholeness?

Personal Application Questions (for breakout groups)

1. Identify the thoughts from your childhood that hinder you from experiencing the love of God in your life.
2. Find the voice of Dr. Jekyll and that Mr. H(i)yde in your mind that you have given rulership to, that speaks loudest to your subconscious. Reverse the volume so that you hear the voice of God over all of them.
3. Prepare, in prayer, daily, for your battle against the enemy who desires to keep you weak and afraid.

Weekly Prayer Target:

1. Pray for the love of Christ to take over your thinking.

2. Pray for strength to confide in your wife and your children about your fears and ask them to do the same as you pray for each other. They, too, have their own fears. Remember, this will not happen overnight. It's a lifetime process.
3. Have the family prepare a flowchart of their fears, and work together to eliminate them. Start with their biggest concern first.

PRAYER

Heavenly Father, I ask You to take me back to those moments, those events in my life where I allowed a doorway to be opened where I received ungodly thoughts, an insecure attitude about myself, and a fear of success. I thank You that I can come to You with my issues and, like the woman who had the issues of blood, You are healing me. Help my family and me address all of the issues that we have that have hindered us from walking in the love that Jesus walked in. I thank You for the revelation of light that You shine on my soul so that I can be the husband, stepfather, and mentor that You have ordained me to be. In Jesus' name, Amen!

CHAPTER

4

GOD ADOPTED YOU

"For ye have not received the spirit of bondage again to fear; but ye have received the Spirit of adoption, whereby we cry, Abba, Father" (Romans 8:15). *"Having predestinated us unto the adoption of children by Jesus Christ to himself, according to the good pleasure of his will"* (Ephesians 1:5). Everybody knows that when Adam and Eve ate the forbidden fruit, they lost direct access to God, which resulted in an *identity crisis*. Because of their sin, God could no longer have direct and personal fellowship with them as He had before. Their new father was Satan.

Let's take a minute to thank our Heavenly Father for sending His Son, Christ, to redeem us from our sinful nature (John 3:16). God loved us so much that He sent His only begotten son to open our blinded eyes so that we could have direct access to Him. When we choose to no longer follow Satan in the spirit of disobedience and follow God in the spirit of obedience, God adopts and makes us heirs with Him and joint heirs with Christ. We are no longer clothed in the shame of our sinful nature. We now are able to come naked before the Lord with holy praise.

The meaning of adoption is: The action or fact of legally taking another's child and bringing it up as one's own. This word becomes powerful when its meaning is applied to you. I am not talking about physical adoption here. My focus here is on the spiritual. You see, like you, David says in Psalm 51:5, "*Behold, I was shapen in iniquity; and in sin did my mother conceive me.*" There are several different ways you can look at this Scripture. All of us were born in a language culture without having any knowledge of how to speak the language. It is learned. It could mean the world of sin that all of us are born in, or you may have been born out of wedlock (Matthew 1:18–25). The word "bastard" (*mamzer*) in Hebrew means "alienate." As we were alienated from God because of Adam's sin, Christ was alienated because of an unwarranted perception that Mary, His mother, had engaged in a sex act with a man other than her espoused husband, Joseph, and became pregnant.

So, as with Israel in Hosea 5:7, "*They have dealt treacherously against the Lord: for they have begotten strange children: now shall a month devour them with their portions,*" sin *alienated* us from God because while we are shaped in iniquity and born with a sinful nature, we are strangers to God, needing to be adopted into His family. Sir, Satan is the destroyer of nations through the destruction of families. If you allow yourself, your wife, and your children to die because of your unwillingness to train, you and your household will be *strangers* to God. Because you choose not to bring them before God by sacrificing your will to honor His, you become *strange* as well.

Ask yourself why David was not included with his brothers when Samuel came to Jesse looking for the next king of Israel (1 Samuel 16:11–13). Hmm! Please remember, like David, Jesus' father wasn't married to Mary in the sense that we considered marriage natural. So, everyone who knew Him (Jesus) looked upon Him as a bastard child as well. The meaning of "bastard" is "illegitimate."[10] Illegitimate means not being recognized as a lawful offspring, specifically, being born of parents who are not married to each other. It is a type of iniquity. If you are looking for a deeper explanation of the word iniquity, I talk about it in my podcast.[11] You just might find it interesting. It means a sin that involves a deliberate and conscious choice to disobey God's commandments or to harm others. Gross injustice, wickedness.[12] Be careful. Like Jesse, what you and others may reject is the very thing that God uses to show Himself mighty.

As we all are "shaped in iniquity and conceived in sin," you no longer have to accept this as your reality if you have been *Born Again* in the Spirit of God. Let me explain. We are bastards in the sense that we were not conceived in the Spirit of Holiness like Christ, which is under the control of God. We were conceived in the spirit of the "lust of the flesh," which is under the control of Satan. Please note I used the word "control," for this deity moves to control you as its host. Also, how many men date a woman when they recognize that they want to spend the rest of their life with her in holy matrimony? If she has children, do they put them first? We tend to look at those children as a by-product of our relationship with their mother. In your mind, they don't belong to you. Have you considered adopting them? God gave you His name! Can you, if she and they are willing, give them your name? Well, I understand that if a biological father is present, that may not happen unless he wants to give up all rights to his child(ren). All children long to belong. It doesn't matter how rebellious they may be; they want to belong. It is one of the 5 tips to strengthen your child's sense of belonging.[13]

You have your work cut out for you. Please remember that some of these children come from Christian families. We may never know the reason they are there, but we do know they need to be covered under the blood of Jesus. As your conversion is complete in Christ, so is theirs. They may never be adopted in the natural, but God will (I John 3:1–2).

THE CRAB

I was watching a nature program the other day on the television, and I was amazed at what the soft-shell crab does in cycles of its life. Crabs

do not have skin or an internal skeleton like human beings and most other mammals do.

Instead of skin and bones, crabs are equipped with an exoskeleton—the external skeleton that exists on the outside of an organism.[14] On the one hand, it greatly benefits the crabs because it enhances leverage for muscular movements and protects internal organs. On the other hand, the main disadvantage of the external skeleton is that it restricts the growth of the animal. The exoskeleton is hard and rigid. So, it does not grow—it cannot grow. Therefore, crabs must shed their old exoskeletons to make room for new ones. Unfortunately, it is not that easy.

Proverbs 28:14 reads, *"Happy is the man that feareth alway: but he that hardeneth his heart shall fall into mischief."* Like the soft-shell crab, we have to know when it is time to molt. We have to know when it is time to come out of our flesh and walk in the Spirit. Spiritual molting is a lifelong process. Too often, we are hindered due to the attacks of the enemy while God is taking us through our spiritual molting process. Your molting is spiritual; however, many men, women, boys, and girls are not looking forward to their spiritual molting process. It is the process of putting the flesh to death.

Because of this, when it is forced onto them, they are subject to come away with broken limes , broken ideas, and a broken faith simply because they fought against the process. Your flesh is your biggest enemy. It doesn't want to be molted. Even though it has become hard and callus, frigid and useless for the Kingdom of God, it doesn't want to die. This is why it is important for you to molt totally out of your past relationships and life experiences so that God can reveal to you a new and more godly way. As you do not belong to yourself, your family does not belong to you. You must give them back to God. You do this by leading the way.

As Jesus warned the Laodicean Church (Revelation 3:14–19), you too cannot be lukewarm. You, as a step-in-father, have to stop straddling the fence. You can no longer be passive about the process. God wants to do a transforming work in you, and it requires your surrender. Surrender to Him, and He will lead you to greener pastures. Too often, we, as men, fight for the rest that God wants to give us. Too often, our focus is on ourselves and not on Him. Too often, we look to receive more than what we are required to and are willing to give: our life. I know, it doesn't seem easy, and it isn't when you are in your flesh. But when you truly surrender to Jesus, it becomes easy. All I can say to you at this point is that you have to molt out of your flesh and embrace your new covering in God's anointing. He, and only He, can show you how to be a step-in-father. He has mastered it. You have been adopted into His family; all you have to do is follow His lead and molt back into His image and likeness.

GENERAL DISCUSSION QUESTIONS (FOR WHOLE GROUPS)

1. Have you considered adoption?
2. If you and your wife or any of the children are not interested in adoption, how will it impact you?
3. How did you feel about the use of the word "bastard"?
4. Why do you think the word "bastard" carries such a negative connotation?
5. Personal Application Questions (for breakout groups)
6. What in your mindset keeps you clinging to your flesh?
7. If you are not molting into the image of God, what might you be molting into?
8. Given the condition of the world today, would you be interested in listing topics that you may need to discuss with your family, e.g., social media and bullying, and incorporate them into your family Bible studies?

Weekly Prayer Target

1. Embrace your adoption.
2. Embrace the adoption of your children from a spiritual perspective.
3. Take a daily spiritual check on your activities during the day to ensure you line up with God's word.
4. Search and find those carnal areas in your life that you must molt out of.

PRAYER

Heavenly Father, I come to you as a sinner saved by Your grace. I know that sometimes I feel that I have it all together, but that is my flesh talking. Help me, Lord. Show me how to put my flesh to death daily so that my adoption into Your Kingdom is assured. As I pursue the molting process by Your Spirit, help me, my wife, and our child(ren) discern the needs of each other in this area. Give me insight into the mindset and attitudes that they may have toward me, each other, and You. You are my Abba, Father, and I surrender all of my fears to Your capable hand. I thank You now for the healing power of Your Word over my home. In Jesus' name, I pray. Amen!

CHAPTER 5

FOR THE TEAM

Ecclesiastes 9:11 reads, *"I returned, and saw under the sun, that the race is not to the swift, nor the battle to the strong, neither yet bread to the wise, nor yet riches to men of understanding, nor yet favor to men of skill; but time and chance happeneth to them all."* Matthew 24:13 reads, *"But he that shall endure unto the end, the same shall be saved."* Please remember that you are not only in a race for your life but, more importantly, you are in a race for the lives of your family (your legacy). To bring them under the rulership of God. You have to become more persistent in the spiritual feeding of your family, regardless of how bankrupt you feel or think. Remember, until you die to yourself and surrender it all to God, you will continue to hinder God's plan for you and for your family.

The crucial element here, and you must come to terms with it, is the fact that your family is your primary ministry. Everything you do should be done to protect your home's emotional and spiritual condition.

You are in a race, and you are in a war; you are required to feed your family the word of God. You must—there is no doubt about it—live a life rich in praise and worship to Yeshua (Jesus), and you should armor up your family for the battle(s) to come. You have been given the *mantel* (the opportunity) and time needed to present your wife and the children before God without a spot, wrinkle, or blemish.

Let's get real here. After the awe-inspiring effects of the honeymoon period have worn away, when the toilet paper isn't on the roll like you want it, the toilet seat is left up, the children aren't responding to your requests as fast as you think they should, you leave your dirty undergarments on the floor, you confess that you think house-cleaning is a woman's job, and she spends more time with her children than with you and your children, etc., etc., etc., you are required to teach in love. Now Matthew 24:13 kicks you in your gut, and you have the rest of your committed life to live and endure God's hand separating you from your flesh and giving you the mindset of Christ.

ENDURANCE

It is stated in Genesis 2:24, "*Therefore shall a man leave his father and his mother, and shall cleave unto his wife: and they shall be one flesh.*" I believe we men have made the physical sex act the climactic event to the "one flesh" scenario expressed in the text.

Let's just take a few minutes and look at *sex* and the word *intercourse*. Intercourse has three distinct meanings:

1. Connection or dealing between persons or groups.
2. Exchange, especially of thoughts or feelings: COMMUNION.
3. Physical, sexual contact between individuals that involves the genitalia of at least one person.

If both you and your wife can somehow focus more on definitions one and two and far less on definition three, you will find that you will understand each other's needs and work to fulfill them.

"Husbands, love your wives, even as Christ also loved the church, and gave himself for it" (Ephesians 5:25). And, *"Wives, submit yourselves unto your own husbands, as unto the Lord"* (Ephesians 5:22). Proverbs 18:22 reads, *"Whoso findeth a wife findeth a good thing, and obtaineth favor of the Lord."* After I had read these Scriptures numerous times, God gave me a revelation. Now check this out. You have to clearly understand and submit yourself to the godly role of a God-fearing husband before you look to find a wife. Some of you reading this want to get married, but you are not yet husband material. You have no idea about the sacrifice you make. You truly have not counted the cost. You are instructed to live a sacrificial life in marriage as Christ has done for His bride, *the Church*. This kind of sacrifice can be even harder for a man entering into a blended family ministry.

For a final thought on this, there are many women who want to get married, but they, too, are not yet wife material. As quiet as it is kept, they are not wife material for anyone. This applies to some of you as well. Sir, you must check your motive for seeking a wife. Is it to honor the ministry of marriage and God, or is it to solely satisfy the carnal urges of your decaying flesh, which is already a stench in the nostrils of God? Count the cost.

Anyway, here is a nugget for you. There are many men who qualify as "husbands," and there are many women who qualify as "wives." The problem is, do you fit together? You should never attempt to take a Ford auto part and affix it to a Lamborghini; the parts just don't fit, and they never will. The question that you must ask yourself is: Is she bone of my bone and flesh of my flesh? Are you *equally yoked*? If you are honest with yourselves, the answer is "no" in numerous cases! You were so focused on the physical aspects of the relationship that you eagerly overlooked and neglected the spiritual/godly standards. "She'll change AFTER we are married" is what we tell ourselves because we have become addicted to the physical due to our submission to secular norms. Stop here and read Proverbs 21:9. This system of man has brought media images of carnal glamour and not spiritual holiness, all in the need to get a quick fix of sex. *You know it can be addictive.* We haven't realized that Satan has us thinking more about the sex act and less about the process of continued godly communication outside the bedroom where you spend the majority of your time. Not just any communication, but the communication that *daily* ushers in the will of God and His presence into your marriage ministry.

DRAMA

Some of you may be asking, "What does all this have to do with Mom's house?" Good question. Please note that you tend to, *you and her*, either set up your home in the image of your parents, or if you had a traumatic experience there, you seek and attempt to set it up in the image you, the individual, have created in your mind. You tend not to work together to establish the foundation and spiritual rudiment of a united home. You both have separate visions of what you want. As it should be clear now that your wife is not your mother, please understand that your ministry is to serve your wife, not the image of your mother. Also, let me remind you once again that your wife's role is not to serve you. It is to help you. Yes, she is there to help you, come along beside you, and make things happen spiritually for both of you and the children. This is not a competition; this is putting God first in all of your family decisions and maximizing your spiritual gifts by joining them together as one.

Here is a question for you. If your mother and your wife were shopping together and were involved in a car accident and sent to different hospitals, which hospital would you visit first? Whom do you put before your wife? Is it your job, friends, social life, sports, television, possessions, or parents? If anything outside of God's will for your life takes precedence over your wife, you have reduced her to a commodity; you exchange her at will for something else that seems to be more precious or holds more *value* to you at that time. In other words, you are not balanced. You sway with your emotions and your feelings. Instead of building, you unknowingly become the wrecking crew. What I want you to see here is that any material thing you have or want that supersedes your unfailing communion with your wife causes you to become an *abomination* to God.

CHILDREN

"... Obtaineth favor from the Lord." We can agree that there are no two children that are alike. Twins demonstrate unique differences. You cannot show favoritism to any of your children, be they biological or blended. Just ask Jacob, Genesis 37:3. If you do, you have lost the race before it gets started. You have the awesome task/responsibility of learning your children's characteristics, their likes, their dislikes, their temperaments, and their spiritual maturity. Now, couple that with the above-mentioned with your wife and yourself.

You have to pace yourself. You have to study the terrain, and you have to become a MacGyver, a man, a husband, and a father who has an extraordinary knack for being an unconventional problem-solver with an extensive bank of spiritual knowledge and understanding that can be best put to use in maturing and saving lives. The spiritual life of your family.

You become the lead minister of the nursery, Children's Church Pastor, Youth Pastor, and Marriage Counselor. God expects nothing less. Luke 14:28–29 reads, *"For which of you, intending to build a tower, sitteth not down first, and counteth the cost, whether he have sufficient to finish it? Lest [perhaps], after he hath laid the foundation, and is not able to finish it, all that behold it begin to mock him."* We tend not to look at the cost of ministering in marriage from a spiritual perspective. It is all placed in the realm of the physical. Sometimes, you may even give it to someone in the five-fold ministry who may not be equipped to counsel you. Marriage isn't about the physical realm; it has and always will be about the spiritual realm. Each child has to be born into the Kingdom of God through your evangelical and discipleship skills. You and only you are the conduit. Are you ready? Even though you are in a blended family, your ministry starts with winning the souls of your children and her children to Christ. It is not the ecclesia's job; it is yours alone and yours together. You are like an apostle, giving birth to a church. Now, mature in it, in Jesus' name.

MISSIONARY

Yes, you are a missionary for the Lord; you are an Apostle for Christ. You have been sent out to preach the gospel to your wife and your children, building a house for God to dwell in.[8] Trust me. They are not going to want to hear from you. Your wife is too busy focusing on her job, on the physical and emotional needs of the children, and on the physical needs of the home. The children, on the other hand, are focused on their father, their media pursuits, and their self-image. If their father is alive and has an active relationship with them, they may just be getting mixed signals or the wrong signals about you from him. And then we have you. Struggling to balance your secular responsibilities against your spiritual ones and being challenged on all fronts. Too many men are compromising their leadership roles in the home in an effort to maintain secular peace. I'm quite sure you will agree that anything with two heads is an abomination and there are many marriages today fitting that description. Oh, by the way, can you tell me where this phrase came from? "A happy wife, a happy life."[15] Some early mention of this phrase seems to have come from a play. Further, the way that most people understand the saying "happy wife, happy life" is that if you want to be content as a *spouse* (husband), you better make sure to do whatever you have to do to keep your wife happy.[16] Even though this phrase may have a hint of truth to it, note that the phrase makes you the bearer of her happiness. If either of you came into the marriage with some unhealthy issues, do not expect your spouse to make you healthy. Trust me, you can't make her happy either, as you both may be dealing with demonic issues that only God can address. Get to work, my friend.

You are no longer living in your parents' house. You are to cleave to your wife, learning and pruning her as you work together to become one. Be in hard pursuit of her for the rest of your days together. Endure to the end. Like a lion, you continuously hunt for her affection. You focus on her needs, not her wants, and you are always reaching out to her in a quest for oneness in mind, body, and spirit. As time goes on, she will bring her children in line under your leadership. *Remember, you have to conquer Satan, not her.* This is why communication—communion—between you two is key. Avoid all negative communion, and always start and end your conversations with *pillow talk*, prayer, and Christ.

COMMUNION

2 Timothy 4:2 reads, "*Preach the word; be instant [diligent] in season, out of season; reprove, rebuke, exhort with all long suffering and doctrine.*" You will know if your wife fits you if she communions with you daily in the Word of God and prayer. The children will also be required to communion because Proverbs 22:6 reads, "*Train up a child in the way he should go: and when he is old, he will not depart from it.*" Not only do you have to commune daily with your wife, but you must also commune daily with the children. God is counting on you.

We talked earlier about the race. When you married this woman and took on the responsibility of being a dad, a step-in-father to her children, you became a team of spiritual Olympic runners. Life experiences together are your training ground. You, by the power of the Spirit of God, have the task of training them to run in the fall, in the spring, in the summer, and in the winters of their lives. Each of you is going to run into quicksand, earthquakes, volcanic eruptions, tsunamis, hail, and snow blizzards, and not at the same time. Each of you will need to learn how to don your life support systems—the

Word of God—in order to support you when you find yourself in situations over your head or adrift in the sea of men and demons. You will have to be the standard that your children attempt to live by. Drugs, alcohol, gender change, sex, and violence are calling out to our youth today. Remember, just because they are in church doesn't mean they are born again. This includes the parents and friends that you and they associate with in church.

Finally, for this chapter, as a team leader, do your children feel that they can talk to you about anything and everything? Their fears, their emotions, what's going on in their schools, what's happening in their bodies? If not, I suggest you slowly take your time here, talk to your wife, and develop a solid plan on how to get them to open up. Remember, they have to become one with you, too.

Are you ready to die for the team?

GROUP DISCUSSION QUESTIONS

Study Discussion Questions (for the whole group)

1. What is the general teaching we are seeking to grasp in this chapter?
2. What changes do we/you need to make in response to the lesson this week (in actions, mindset, etc.)?
3. Describe the positive and negative effects of media on the family today.
4. Give some examples where you see the ecclesia (families) missing the call to be holy.
5. How has the infiltration of world views negatively impacted you, the family, and the ecclesia?

Personal Application Questions (for breakout groups)

1. What did the Lord impress upon your heart as you read this chapter?
2. Are you finding it increasingly difficult to protect your wife and your children by fully following God in today's culture?
3. What are some of the challenges you are facing?
4. When you see all that is coming against your family, do you accept or resist it? In what ways?
5. In what ways are you doing a little bit of both?

Weekly Prayer Targets

1. Pray that God will give you the eyes of faith to see beyond what you are experiencing today.

2. Cry out to God for the family to return to Him and His ways as He does a deep pruning and uprooting work in your home.

3. Pray that the family would hear the call to awaken, resist the world's ways, and mature in their faith to be more than conquerors in Jesus Christ.

PRAYER

Heavenly Father, in the mighty name of Jesus, I come to You in humble submission to Your perfect will in my life. It is because of Your grace, Your mercy, and Your favor upon me that I come to You at this time in prayer and supplication for myself, my wife, and our child(ren). I ask now that You examine my heart and renew the right spirit within us so that we may be the righteous seed planted in the vineyard of mankind, bearing much fruit.

I seek deliverance in our lives from being a vehicle used by Satan to sew discard and hatred amongst each other. It is because of You and only because of You that we have an example of how we should be living. Christ was sent into this world to illustrate to us how to live humbled lives, seeking peace with all whom we encounter. We know that this is Your purpose for us and that Your desire is for us to walk daily in this purpose, the ministry of marriage, and with You. You have designed for each of us, from the foundation of the world, Your spirit of warfare against the enemy of our soul, and we submit to Your purpose for our lives.

SELF REFLECTION

Well, I would say this is the end, but in truth, it is your beginning. Take this opportunity to create your own prayer as you work for the team. You may want to have the whole family create their own. It can be a tool to keep each of you focused on God. Remember, as each of you continues to mature in your spiritual walk, your prayers will change.

_____

_____

_____

_____

_____

MY PRAYER FOR YOU

Father, I ask that each man reading this book will move into a state of repentance. Christ told us in Matthew 4:17a to *"Repent: for the kingdom of heaven is at hand."* Open their eyes to all of the areas in their life that they need to repent and die to. Holy Spirit, they need You now more than ever before. Their spirit is willing, but their flesh is weak. I thank You for calling them out for such great work, molding and shaping the direction of these children into Your image. I am grateful for this opportunity. They will finish their assignment.

CONCLUSION

For the purpose of clarity, if you have children and are planning to marry a woman with children, or if you have children and have married a woman with children, it is imperative that you work at gauging the mental and emotional prospects of your union. Now isn't the time to be self-centered. The world system has given us, in many cases, incorrect scenarios of what a man is. It is self-centeredness. Men rule! But let me be clear here. You can't rule anything outside of yourself if you haven't learned how to rule the inner you by submitting to God.

Your role as a man is just that: a role. Your role as a father is just that: a role. The problem is that we don't have many godly male role models. This means that even though you may look like a man from a physical perspective, what are you doing on your spiritual side to mature into a Godman? Yes, you can do great things outside yourself to show your manhood, but what are you doing on the inside to show your godhood? In being a step-in-father, living out your godhood becomes more paramount for you, as you, like Christ, are grafting the nature of God in yourself as well as in the children that you are training to be like Him. Yes, I said, "like Him," not "like you."

I believe, too often, we as godly men focus too much on the physicality of what the perception of a man is and miss out on the great opportunities to simply be a "Man of God." Be honest with yourself here. No one needs to know but God. Let me give you an example by looking at Moses, Numbers 12:3, *"Now the man Moses was very meek, above all the men which were upon the face of the earth."* Depressed, in mind (gentle) or circumstances (needy, especially saintly): humble, lowly, meek, poor.[17] Let me take a few minutes here and explain this Scripture. I don't want you to look at the word "depressed" in a negative way ever again. We need to first ask ourselves, "What is it that needs to be depressed?" I'm glad you asked. Moses did not have a good hold on his temper.

Remember, he lost his temper and premeditatively killed a man (Exodus 2:11–12). After fleeing from Egypt and running into a desert experience for forty years, he was able to bring that temper under control and not explode like a volcano and spew out hot ash on those who offended him. Trust me; there will be times in your marriage when you will feel you have been offended by your wife and by the child(ren). It is not a feeling; you will be offended by them. After his desert (*his wilderness*) experience, Moses learned how to be gentle (*meek*) in all circumstances of his life. Like Moses, God is working on your behalf to bring you through. You will not be able to do it yourself; however, in order to get to the promised land, you must be obedient to the perfect will God has for you and your family. Death to self is your beginning. He is the light in your darkness.

Moses' meekness was due to his willingness to submit to the likeness and image of God in all of his actions. As with every man, woman, boy, and girl, we all have to become needy of the presence of God in our everyday lives. If we ever feel we don't need Him, we will stop pursuing Him; we won't care to obtain His love and forgiveness because we will be too busy loving ourselves and feeling no need to be forgiven for our shortcomings. When this happens, we stop loving our family, and the love that we selfishly desire is a desire to have our carnal wants fulfilled, neglecting the godly needs that we, as priests of the home, are mandated to fulfill in the lives of our family.

Like Moses, as the under-shepherd of Israel before God, you are the under-shepherd of your family. As God prepared Moses for his earthly assignment, you have been called out by God for an earthly assignment. Any complaints that you may muster up to deflate your ability to fulfill this assignment are unwarranted. Moses had help. You do, too. Your help is your help meet. Before I go any further, please, please, do not neglect her in the training process. Remember, the child in each of you still needs training, and you both must be sensitive to that fact. She is your Jethro. Pay attention to her truth, not to your feelings. As you have been adopted into the family of God, you now have the joyful assignment of under-shepherding your children and hers and leading them to greener pastures in Christ. I congratulate you on your ministry. Study to show yourself approved. Remember this. Moses had to leave Egypt, and he journeyed to Midian, a desert country south of Judah. My point here is to reiterate the fact that Moses left Egypt, and forty years later, he was directed to return and free God's children. Whatever transpired in your previous relationships, marriage, or otherwise (your Egypt), it is my prayer that you truly hear the voice of God as you enter into and become a blended family. Not only do you have to crucify your physical past, but, more importantly, you have to crucify your spiritual past as well. You cannot move forward in Christ until you stop bathing in your past. Also, you are not there to force the children or your bride to love you. You are there to show them how to love God by being the best example you can be of that love. Like Eve and Adam in the garden, the moment you take your eyes off Christ, you begin to descend into a carnal pit that will choke the godly life out of you. Thank God right here and right now for giving you the strength to ascend to the spiritual height you have been called to by Him.

Now, as Moses had a rite of passage, you do, too. Remember, men, Jesus tells you in Matthew 5:5, *"Blessed are the meek: for they shall inherit the earth."*

Rite of Passage: An official ceremony or informal activity that marks an important stage or occasion in a person's life, especially becoming an adult.[18]

Here are six things that differentiate a man from a boy.[6]

1. Worship

    a. All of life is about worship. The boy needs to know this from an early age.

    b. Rite of Passage? Sometime a little after the boy repents and believes in Jesus, gather a small group of men that you respect and that he knows. Ask these men to tell your son about the Love of Christ and what being a Christian man is.

2. Work

    a. Include your son in as much work as you can . From a young age, he should be acquainted with work.

    b. Rite of Passage? During his teenage years, use a "Titanic" task that seems impossible, and assign the work to him. This may be clearing out and burning trees or demolishing a house. Any job that requires persistence, plodding, sweat, and likely blood will do. When the project is completed, celebrate it and bestow a reward (Gift) upon him.

3. Protect

    a. Require your son to work out and/or take martial arts or self-defense training.

    b. Sons need to be trained and prepared to use and take care of firearms. When he turns 21, he should be ready to conceal carry.

    c. Rite of Passage? Beat you in wrestling. Complete a skills course with a variety of different firearms.

4. Provide

    a. Sons need to understand how money works. He will be required to make and manage money.

    b. He also will need to be prepared to provide for other needs that being a head of household demands.

    c. Rite of passage? One month of hunting/fishing for everything he eats. No food should be provided except what he can provide for himself.

5. Lead

    a. Our sons are born leaders. God demands that of them. He is built to overcome adversity. We must tell them this.

    b. Rite of passage? Prepare and lead a week-long outdoor adventure/survival trip. The father has spent his life leading the son; now it is time for the son to lead the trip for himself and his father.

6. Love

   a. Love should be the standard MO of the household. The father should lead the way with this.

   b. Rite of passage? When it becomes obvious that the son is learning to deny himself before God and men, a ceremony is fitting. This should include a valuable gift, a good meal, and a good drink, tailored to the young man. The father should speak to his son about sacrifice as we follow in the footsteps of our Master.

SCRIPTURE REFERENCES

INTRODUCTION

1. Genesis 1:28 KJV
2. Matthew 1:19 KJV
3. Matthew 1:20 KJV
4. 2 Corinthians 5:7 KJV
5. Luke 2:24 KJV
6. Leviticus 12:8 KJV
7. Matthew 1:18 KJV
8. Matthew 1:16–17 KJV
9. Matthew 1:18–19 KJV
10. Matthew 1:19 KJV
11. Proverbs 22:6 KJV
12. Hosea 5:7 KJV

CHAPTER 1

WHO ARE YOU?

1. Proverbs 20:5 KJV
2. Proverbs 20:18 KJV

3. Genesis 2:18 KJV
4. Psalm 51:5 KJV
5. Philippians 2:25 KJV
6. Ephesians 5:25 KJV
7. Galatians 5:22–23a KJV
8. Luke 14:12–19 KJV
9. Proverbs 30:10–31 KJV

CHAPTER 2

I'M GOING TO MY MOTHER'S HOUSE

1. Genesis 3:16 KJV
2. Mark 12:30–31 KJV
3. Genesis 9:25 KJV
4. Genesis 3:16 KJV
5. John 8:12 KJV
6. Matthew 5:14 KJV
7. 1 Kings 18 KJV
8. Judges 16; 17
9. Genesis 2:24 KJV
10. 2 Timothy 3:1–5 KJV
11. Ephesians 5:25 KJV

12. Ephesians 6:4 KJV

13. Philippians 2:12 KJV

14. Ezekiel 3:17 KJV

15. Ezekiel 8:9 KJV

CHAPTER 3

ALL BY MYSELF?

1. Matthew 22:37–40 KJV

2. Ephesians 2:8 KJV

3. James 4:4 KJV

4. Luke 4:13 KJV

5. Isaiah 54:17 KJV

CHAPTER 4

GOD ADOPTED YOU

1. Romans 8:15 KJV

2. Ephesians 1:5 KJV

3. John 3:16 KJV

4. Psalm 51:5 KJV

5. Matthew 1:18–25 KJV

6. Hosea 5:7 KJV

7. 1 Samuel 16:11–13 KJV

8. 1 John 3:1–2 KJV

9. Proverbs 28:14 KJV

10. Revelation 3:14–19 KJV

CHAPTER 5

FOR THE TEAM

1. Ecclesiastes 9:11 KJV

2. Matthew 24:13 KJV

3. Genesis 2:24 KJV

4. Ephesians 5:25 KJV

5. Ephesians 5:22 KJV

6. Proverbs 18:22 KJV

7. Proverbs 21:9 KJV

8. Proverbs 8:35 KJV

9. Genesis 37:3 KJV

10. Luke 14:28–29 KJV

11. 2 Timothy 4:2 KJV

12. Proverbs 22:6 KJV

CONCLUSION

1. Numbers 12:3 KJV

2. Exodus 2:11–12 KJV

3. Matthew 5:5 KJV

REFERENCES

INTRODUCTION

1. Quiet Leadership: A Profile of Joseph, Father of Jesus. http://www.word-smith.info/biographies/quiet-leadership , 2005.

2. SmartFamilies,RonL.Deal,M.MFT,http://www.smartstepfamilies.com/view/statistics. Last modified, April 2014.

3. https://smartstepfamilies.com/smart-help/marriage-family-stepfamily-statistics

CHAPTER 1

WHO ARE YOU?

4. Dr. Reynald J. Williams, I, *The Garden of Your Mind*, Enoch Publishing and Enterprises, 2015.

CHAPTER 2

I'M GOING TO MY MOTHER'S HOUSE

5. Wellington Boone, *Your Wife Is Not Your Mother*, Doubleday, March 1999.

6. Wellington Boone, Your Wife Is Not Your Mother. Page 77. Doubleday, March 1999.

7. Natalie Nichols Gillespie, The Stepfamily Survival Guide. Page 53. Revell, 2004.

CHAPTER 3

ALL BY MYSELF?

8. https://www.therapistaid.com/therapy-article/what-is-loneliness

9. Dr. Reynald J. Williams, I, *The Garden of Your Mind*, Enoch Publishing and Enterprises, 2015.

CHAPTER 4

GOD ADOPTED YOU

10. https://www.merriam-webster.com/dictionary/bastard

11. YouTube, Garden of Your Mind Podcast

12. https://www.merriam-webster.com/dictionary/iniquity

13. https://belongingnetwork.com/article/belonging-matters-tips-to-strengthen-your-childs-sense-of-belonging.

14. https://aquariumbreeder.com/crabs-and-molting-process/

CHAPTER 5

FOR THE TEAM

15. https://svenstudios.com/2023/08/the-science-behind-happy-wife-happy-life-is-it-true/#:~:text=It's%20a%20phrase%20that's%20been,in%20Abilene%2C%20Texas%20in%201958.

16. https://www.regain.us/advice/marriage/is-the-saying-happy-wife-happy-life-true-why-it-could-be-dangerous-for-your-marriage

CONCLUSION

17. Strong's Exhaustive Concordance of the Bible, Hebrew reference, pg. 90–6035, 6041.

18. https://dictionary.cambridge.org/dictionary/english/rite-of-passage

19. https://goodmenproject.com/guy-talk/seven-things-that-make-a-boy-a-man-mneo-cmtt/

20. https://themajestysmen.com/gospelpost/rights-of-passage/

www.ingramcontent.com/pod-product-compliance
Lightning Source LLC
Chambersburg PA
CBHW071738090426
42738CB00011B/2523